Notes on Education

Howie Soucek

… a man's reach should exceed his grasp,
or what's a heaven for?
—"Andrea Del Sarto," Robert Browning

TEACH Services, Inc.
P U B L I S H I N G
www.TEACHServices.com ● (800) 367-1844

Copyright © 2015 Howie Soucek
Copyright © 2015 TEACH Services, Inc.
ISBN-13: 978-1-4796-0454-8 (Paperback)
ISBN-13: 978-1-4796-0455-5 (ePub)
ISBN-13: 978-1-4796-0456-2 (mobi)
Library of Congress Control Number: 2014951049

Ver. 2a

Published by

TEACH Services, Inc.
P U B L I S H I N G
www.TEACHServices.com • (800) 367-1844

Table of Contents

Introduction 5

Chapter 1   Organize for Instruction 11

Chapter 2   Incentives for Performance and Teamwork 21

Chapter 3   From Technicians to Professionals 27

Chapter 4   Professional Responsibility 37

Chapter 5   Meaningful Attention Versus Mass Production . . 41

Chapter 6   What Did You Expect? 47

Chapter 7   A Real Teacher 53

Chapter 8   Teach Them How to Learn 63

Chapter 9   Let's Talk About Right and Wrong 79

Chapter 10   Our Moral Imperative 85

Introduction

My concerns about K-12 education in the United States developed during the time I was a middle school teacher in the 1970s. Although I was part of an exciting team of professionals at the time and we were producing good results, I saw a diversity of children full of potential at every level but retarded in their progress by the hidden agendas of some of the local powerful, by widespread apathy or ignorance among too many adults in the community, and by the inertia and incompetence of distant governmental bureaucracies, state-level committees, and publishing houses—out of touch or unconcerned with the realities dwelling in my classroom, my school, and my community.

At the same time, books such as *Crisis in the Classroom* (by Charles E. Silberman, 1970) and news stories about our lackluster academic performance within the international community added to my concerns and made it clear that the problems I saw locally represented in only a small way a national plague of educational deficiency.

The condition of education in the United States continued to decline during that decade, and in 1981 the U.S. Secretary of Education created the National Commission on Excellence in Education and directed it to present a report on the quality of education in America. The report, *A Nation at Risk: The Imperative for Educational Reform*, was produced in April of 1983. To get a feel for the gravity of our problems in education as reported by our own government at the time, consider the opening two paragraphs of the report:

Our Nation is at risk. Our once unchallenged pre-eminence in commerce, industry, science, and technological innovation is being overtaken by competitors throughout the world. This report is concerned with only one of the many causes and dimensions of the problem, but it is the one that undergirds American prosperity, security, and civility. We report to the American people that while we can take justifiable pride in what our schools and colleges have historically accomplished and contributed to the United States and the well-being of its people, the educational foundations of our society are presently being eroded by a rising tide of mediocrity that threatens our very future as a Nation and a people. What was unimaginable a generation ago has begun to occur—others are matching and surpassing our educational attainments.

If an unfriendly foreign power had attempted to impose on America the mediocre educational performance that exists today, we might well have viewed it as an act of war. As it stands, we have allowed this to happen to ourselves. We have even squandered the gains in student achievement made in the wake of the Sputnik challenge. Moreover, we have dismantled essential support systems which helped make those gains possible. We have, in effect, been committing an act of unthinking, unilateral educational disarmament.

A "rising tide of mediocrity"—That was the incendiary phrase that stimulated so much resonance among the best teachers I knew at the community level, raising our hopes that a nationwide tidal wave of concern and constructive action would surely result from such an obvious need. And yet in spite of this, and in spite of the limited changes that were allowed to be put into place, the product of our systems of education remained mediocre over the following decade.

Indeed, the very title of *Public Education: An Autopsy* (by Myron Lieberman, 1993) seemed but another milepost in an insidious and dreadful journey our nation was continuing nearly a quarter-century after I had begun teaching. Now let us flash forward to the present.

Consider that we permit our government to amass a gigantic financial debt, we tolerate a dreadful decay of our national infrastructure, we allow a dangerous overdependence on oil—especially foreign oil; and we remain acquiescent about inadequate protections against environmental disasters, a lack of investment in alternative energy sources, a stretched military, weakened environmental protections, and a lack of conservation of natural resources (especially clean water).

And last but first… a gross lack of investment in education. *Indeed, our most reprehensible neglect is that we have refused to insist that through effective education our children at least receive the tools they will need to address for themselves the host of problems that we are leaving them.*

We have only to ask the business leaders in our own communities if they are concerned about high school graduates who have trouble filling out a job application, who cannot speak or listen well, who are unable to compose a coherent document, who possess poor problem-solving and project skills, who do not know how to present themselves well in a business environment, and who lack the motivation to attend to tasks well.

And if what our own business leaders are telling us at the local level is incredible, give read to the first two sentences of the Executive Summary of a national report titled *Are They Really Ready To Work?* published late in 2006:

> The future U.S. workforce is here—and it is woe-
> fully ill-prepared for the demands of today's (and

tomorrow's) workplace. So say employers in a unique study by The Conference Board, Corporate Voices for Working Families, Partnership for 21st Century Skills, and the Society for Human Resource Management, which looks at the readiness of new entrants to the workforce.

To bring us up to date with the time of this writing (2008), consider that "research findings show that U.S. HR professionals and employers are unsatisfied with the skills of new entrants to the workforce and concerned that the future workforce will not be able to compete on the global stage." This evaluation is by way of *Workplace Visions*, No. 2, 2008, a publication of the Society for Human Resource Management. By our inaction, how can we continue to deny such a continuous volume of the proverbial handwriting on the wall over such a period of time?

Of course there are some great youngsters coming out of our schools! What is frightening, however, is the alarming proportion of graduates who are ill-prepared to perform well in a job, who have no concept of contributing to their community or society through intelligent civic activities and volunteerism, and who lack a sense of responsibility to *instill* a sense of responsibility, cooperation, diligence, perseverance, foresight, and reliability in their offspring.

In an effort to at least vent myself on this matter (if not make a difference), I wrote a series of letters on education in the 1980s. Having done little with the letters for years, I only recently decided to publish them. And what a sad commentary it is that when I reviewed my years-old writing, I found little to change.

In too many communities the status quo (and its loyal comrades lethargy and hopelessness) reign supreme. But every once in awhile a news story appears about a school and its students in dire straits, with a high dropout rate, rampant disciplinary problems, and low academic performance, which, when a dynamic and passionate leader and team are put into place along with the necessary autonomy and support, achieve sweeping and dramatic improvements within a couple years—and the students are happier, too. All this—achieved without regard to the socioeconomic status of the students.

This begs the question: Why can't this happen everywhere? And the answer is that it *can* if only enough leaders with enough power in the community have the will to *encourage* it to happen and if a critical mass of others in the community step up to make the large and small contributions required to *make* it happen.

The point of my writing is to suggest that this can be executed only at the community level. There is no deus ex machina, and there never was—certainly not when my Dad carried his lunch pail and a clean slate to his one-room schoolhouse each day when he was a boy. Back then, if you did not take care of things yourself in your own community, they did not get taken care of. If you wanted to play a game of baseball, you used saved-up string wound tightly to make a ball while someone else used a knife on a stick to make a bat. You were resourceful by nature. In our time by contrast, too much comes too easily.

Today we have allowed ourselves to become overly dependent on the government and other large, distant entities, thus sacrificing our self-reliance and shirking our own responsibilities in the process. We have even externalized our financial means to our ends, with average credit card debt in the area of $8000. Look next at the national debt—a disgrace. Then look at our children: The tendency is to follow our example, which does not bode well for our nation. Who says that we are not teaching our children? Totally outsourcing their education is in itself perhaps our most harmful lesson to them.

In each section of my notes, I describe a different area of my concern about education, along with some suggestions for improvement at the local level that can be considered by everyone in almost any community. Make no mistake—this writing is no black box program that can be wired in and turned on to provide a great program of education. Instead, *this book is intended to be a catalyst to initiate action within the community and a starting place for a discussion of ideas as to how the community can best pursue its goals for improvement.*

There will be political, parental, school system, and legal challenges to overcome at every turn; for the powers of self-interest and of the status quo are immense. But if we allow ourselves to continue as we have been, we will doom our children's future—whilst blaming everyone but our individual selves all along the way.

I truly hope that everything we do, even if in bits and pieces over time, will have as its purpose the best interests of our children, who have long been victimized at the hands of our misplaced priorities. Our children are our future (or perhaps more aptly, we are our children's future) and if we continue to fail them—well, how can we abide ourselves?

Chapter 1

Organize for Instruction

Most school systems tend to be bureaucratic in structure and function. Organizational style is typically "top-down," with teachers very much left out of the decision-making process. Indeed, a school system superintendent once characterized the teacher-administration relationship as "labor-management." And what a shame it is that so many teachers across our nation accordingly see a need to be "unionized." In this style of organization, the division between the administration and the teachers prevents effective communication, and it diverts educational energy away from the children.

If someone really cared enough to examine the structure and function of the school system (by conducting extensive, non-threatening conversations with school personnel), the discoveries would be made that

- school organizations tend not to provide meaningful incentives, recognition or career development for school personnel; teachers' views are typically not sought out; simply put, teachers generally are not treated as professionals; coincidentally, too many teachers do not behave as professionals;

- there are too many lackluster and even incompetent teachers in our children's classrooms; they numb and alienate many young minds, they detract from educational progress, and their tolerated presence frustrates caring teachers; administrators often fail to do an adequate job of performance evaluation, coaching, and developing lackluster teachers; administrators lack the resources and/or lack the courage to rid the system of incompetence;
- quality teachers too often are frustrated and stifled by administrative ineptness, politics, and trifling applications of authority;
- too many things are done only for appearances and are not meaningful;
- there is little effective communication between the various layers of the organization;
- individuals throughout the organization tend to feel isolated and accordingly self-centered, defensive, or helpless;
- groups (ex. science teachers, seventh grade teachers, office personnel, coaching staff, special services personnel) too often fail to work cooperatively;
- enthusiasm, innovations and even day-to-day efficiencies are suppressed by established policies, procedures, time constraints and failures in communication.
- decisions about curriculum, scheduling, class size, instruction and the like are too often driven by factors other than what is in the best interests of children;
- *the system is highly resistant to change; there is no place for debate or questioning; teachers have been trained to walk on egg shells; the status quo reigns.*

"Teachers" should be considered to be the real professionals on educational matters. They should be key players in determining educational policies, procedures, curriculum, environment, materials and methodology. "Administrators" should support teachers by facilitating, coordinating, supplying teachers' needs, maintaining plant and equipment, and being responsible for truly extracurricular items.

Teachers, guidance and special services personnel, and administrators should all work together as a unified team with a focus always upon the best interests of the children. To whatever extent "we-they" actions and attitudes prevail within the system, children will lose out. My notion of an effective school system organization is as follows:

I. INTERDISCIPLINARY DELIVERY OF INSTRUCTION: Classroom teachers should be formed into interdisciplinary groups. If our goal is to prepare young people for an adult world full of large and small challenges, most of which cut across a variety of skill and knowledge areas at once, it seems to be logical that our instruction in school should be more integrated and coordinated across the academic disciplines.

There should be more history woven into English literature; more grammar, spelling and composition in history; more science and math in physical education; certainly, there should be more reading, vocabulary, and writing woven into *every* subject. Students should understand that success in any significant enterprise is the result of a coordinated, "interdisciplinary" effort that draws upon a complexity of skills and understanding.

Further, students should be encouraged to work cooperatively in large and small groups as opportunities arise, if for no other reason than to prepare for a job with a company that is successful because its people work well together and make sound decisions by consensus.

Indeed, teachers should provide the model for this in how they work together to plan excellent, coordinated instruction. Interdisciplinary groups would meet each week to discuss current issues and group objectives and planning. The mindset within the group would be that of a team with a mission. Importantly, teachers would be vested with decision-making authority appropriate to their professional status.

II. EDUCATION TECHNICIANS: The current concept of individual "teacher aides" would be dropped. Instead, each interdisciplinary group would have available to it a quantity of education technicians sufficient to provide support services for the teachers in the group. Education technicians would not have classroom duties unless there was a special need on occasion. Instead, they would support the group by providing word processing, photocopying, grade averaging, processing recorded dictation, record keeping and similar services. Skill with a PC and appropriate software would be obvious requisite skills for the education technician. Grading objective tests, performing light research, and handling various school communications would be additional duties of the education technician.

I am not talking about something extra or "nice" for the teachers. The fact is that teachers are currently saddled with an enormous clerical/paperwork load which takes away from the time available for the professional responsibilities of innovation, planning, thorough instruction, and comprehensive student evaluation. This kind of support is standard in any true "profession"; why not for teachers?

III. MASTER TEACHER: Leadership for the interdisciplinary group would be provided by a master teacher. This person would have a light class load in order to allow time to observe teacher performance, counsel with teachers during planning periods, meet with other master teachers and administrators, and conduct R&D activities.

The master teacher would have the responsibility to supervise teachers in the group and to conduct their performance appraisals. (It seems highly unlikely to me that one or two administrators can do an effective job of observing and evaluating the performance of a group of people the size of which it takes to staff a whole school.) Too, including master teachers in the organization would provide an important career growth and development opportunity for capable teachers.

IV. HEADMASTER: The master teachers would report to the headmaster of the school as would the administrative principal. This means that the chief person in authority at the school would be an instruction-based person. Educational instruction and learning, after all, are what a school should be all about.

Cafeteria service, janitorial services, plant and equipment maintenance, accounting, purchasing, security, safety, providing teacher supplies, and the like are subordinate services provided by people who report to the administrative principal, who in turn would report to the headmaster.

The headmaster would also supervise the school's guidance, special education, physical education and vocational education functions and ensure that the school's overall instructional program is coordinated and balanced.

With an ever-present emphasis on enhancements and development, the headmaster would meet regularly with the master teachers as a team in planning and implementing the best possible instructional program for the children. The headmaster would evaluate the performance of the master teachers and would also have a consulting role in the performance appraisal of classroom teachers.

V. DIRECTOR OF INSTRUCTION: All the headmasters in the school system would report to the system director of instruction. The director of instruction would coordinate, inspire and guide the system's program of instruction. Perhaps a third of this person's time would be spent observing and working with instructional teams out in the schools. This person would also have a consulting role in the performance appraisal of master teachers.

An ASSISSTANT DIRECTOR OF INSTRUCTION could provide support with educational programs and be responsible for the recruitment and (just as important) the retention of quality instructional and guidance personnel. Responsibility for the *selection* of new personnel would be divided equally amongst the director of instruction, the appropriate headmaster, and the appropriate master teacher.

The great importance of the effective recruitment, selection, orientation, development, and retention of quality personnel for the school system cannot be overemphasized. These are among the first areas of administrative responsibility that should be carefully examined, as the needs for improvement in most school systems are great indeed.

As a couple of examples, consider that the use of mentoring and of exit interviews in too many systems (if they use them at all) amount to meaningless exercises that accomplish nothing more than to allow an administrator to say, "Oh, yes, we do conduct those activities." *There is too much done for show in education, and worse, there are too many who too easily nod in acceptance when presented with flimsy evidence of substantive efforts.*

Let us combine and take a closer look at these two examples. Imagine a motivated person entering a school system as a new teacher—a new teacher who asks for but is given no guidance or support, and whose supervisor does not so much as poke his head in the doorway to see how things are going. This teacher provides excellent instruction and classroom management, but is left to languish alone with her daily smorgasbord of challenges and obstacles.

This is but one way to discourage a good teacher, who subsequently decides to resign at the end of the school year. The bitter icing on this bitter cake is that no supervisor and no administrator in the entire school system expresses any concern that she is leaving, wants to understand the factors in her decision to leave, or even thanks her for the contribution she has made that year.

This kind of preventable loss of excellent talent is absolutely inexcusable, leaving the children once again as the victims of our adult ineptness. Someone like an assistant director of instruction should have the retention of good teachers among the highest priorities, and this requires preventive intelligence-gathering through mentoring programs and effective supervision. If a teacher resigns in spite of that, the least the school system should do in order to minimize such losses in the future is to find out the real reasons involved—perhaps best through a third party.

If good teachers are difficult to retain, they can be even more difficult to recruit. Yet, too many school systems give insufficient attention to the development of effective recruiting strategies, selection procedures (especially interviewing), and orientation programs. Are school systems asking for help with this? Are human resource professionals in the community offering help? If they offer help, are school system administrations accepting it?

Also reporting to the director of instruction would be the ADMINISTRATIVE SUPERINTENDENT, in charge of system-wide matters such as payroll, bus routes, capital projects, bus maintenance, purchasing, and the like.

The director of instruction would be the chief spokesman for the school system in the community and would work to promote large and small partnerships with education throughout the community. The director of instruction would keep abreast of state and federal legislation and judicial system activities affecting education and would play a dynamic role in placing educational concerns at the forefront to the greatest extent possible at local, state and national levels.

VI. SCHOOL BOARD: The school board would include one master teacher from the system amongst its voting members. This individual would serve a one-year term and be selected by the director of instruction from the nominations of the headmasters. It is important for the school board to receive insights directly from a professional in the front lines of education. Those who argue that the school board should limit itself to high-level matters of policy and budget and not be informed and concerned about cumulative day-to-day issues in the classroom are flat wrong.

In fact, there should be a requirement that school board members visit system schools, unannounced, frequently enough as to have a good sense of the effectiveness of the school environment. Occasional meetings with school staff would be good also, as would meetings with student leadership groups and parents.

With such information in hand, the school board will have a better grasp of the detail in the big picture across the system that can be combined with the information fed to it by the system administration and thus be in a better position to promote the education interests of the system within the community—and better protect it from harmful political agendas as well.

Another small example of an initiative a school board could make to begin to close its distance from the real world in which teachers live would be to require a closed-session meeting with teachers who are terminating employment. This would allow the board to gather intelligence that can help reduce avoidable losses and improve policies and procedures that affect the ability of teachers to do their jobs well. At the least, exit interviews should be conducted by a true HR professional or someone independent of the school system power structure, with the results reported to the school board.

We must guard against a school board acting as an isolated figurehead governance rather than as an involved, dynamic oversight body—and against a legacy opportunity for would-be leaders rather than the best vehicle possible for individuals to make a meaningful difference for our children.

The point with all this is that the way people in any enterprise are organized and allowed to function determines the lines and levels of authority and communication within the organization. People must be organized in such a way as to best utilize the talents of everyone in the organization and to achieve the overall goals of the organization.

While a top-down management system may be necessary in a military operation, it is in education a restraint against innovation, against enthusiasm, and against true professionalism. We must unleash and embrace our teachers.

Especially, the design and function of the school system organization must close the communication gap that exists between classroom teachers and those who determine policy and administer programs for the system.

Chapter 2

Incentives for Performance and Teamwork

As a place to begin, consider the salary program most school systems currently use. Such programs have a "salary schedule" with a set number of increasing steps or levels providing payment solely on the basis of the number of years of experience the teacher has. The value of such a program is to be found in its simplicity and in its recognition that a number of teachers will improve their performance as they gain experience.

The damaging effects of such a salary program, however, far outweigh the benefits. First, an insidious drop in performance develops with the security and comfort that some teachers derive from knowing that their work performance and that of the school system as a whole will have little impact, if any, upon their salary. Compounding this is the abhorrent fact that an outstanding teacher receives the same monetary recognition as a lackluster teacher with the same seniority.

Such a salary program removes from an otherwise aspiring teacher any sense of control over his own career growth and development. Such a salary program is demeaning to teachers who would otherwise think of themselves as professionals with high performance that translates into tangible recognition. Such a salary program becomes one of several burnout factors over time for many of our best teachers.

The portion of college graduates today who are looking for a "job" is declining. Instead, more are searching for a rewarding and exciting career opportunity. Young professionals today want challenging work; but they also want a work environment that allows them to exercise judgment and to make a meaningful contribution to the overall organization; they expect meaningful recognition for excellent performance; and they will be most attracted to an organization that provides this recognition by way of a performance-based salary and also by way of career growth and development opportunities over time.

School systems that understand this and alter their salary program accordingly will have a strong advantage in both the recruitment and retention of top quality talent. My recommendation is in three parts:

A. Career Growth and Development

First, the structure of the salary program should be one which provides the opportunity for career growth and development. There could be four levels, or grades, through which a teacher's career could progress. Each promotion would normally provide a significant jump in salary. Each grade would have its own minimum and maximum salaries, which would overlap a bit with adjacent grades.

An inexperienced teacher could begin as a *JUNIOR TEACHER*. After two years, depending upon performance, the individual would receive a promotion to *PROFESSIONAL TEACHER*. The individual would remain at this level until and unless his experience and performance warranted a promotion to *SENIOR TEACHER*. A junior teacher would be mentored by a senior teacher.

If either a professional teacher or a senior teacher demonstrates both excellent instruction and high ability and interest in supervisory responsibility, then a promotion to *MASTER TEACHER* would be in order as the opportunity arises. The master teacher would supervise and be fully responsible for a group of teachers.

At every point along the way in this career growth process, an individual teacher's career development is an important responsibility of the school system, in concert with the interests and capabilities of the teacher.

Rather than limiting this to a compliance with state-mandated re-certification credits, the master teacher, based on conversations with the teacher, should seek out education and training experiences that will best enhance the career development interests and needs of the teacher.

Indeed, as it is the teacher's responsibility to communicate needs for support, it is the system's responsibility to garner the resources needed to support and nourish the teacher's needs.

B. Incentives for Teaming and Self-Responsibility

The traditional salary schedule should be eliminated entirely. Each teacher should receive an annual increase that, within the budgetary "pot," would be determined up to a third by the attainment of school system goals, such as minimizing the drop-out rate; up to a third by the attainment of team/department goals, such as innovative instructional programs or professional development and training activities; and up to a third by the individual's performance appraisal results.

With such a salary program, not only would a teacher's individual performance play a role in his annual raise, but there would also be a strong incentive for the teacher to make a meaningful contribution to his team/department. Teamwork is further enhanced as individual teachers and teams strive to help the overall school system reach its goals.

Instead of salary being based solely on seniority, then, it should be based on performance, cooperation, and the attainment of clearly understood goals. And guess who the beneficiaries will be?

C. Effective Performance Management

The third part of my recommendation addresses the need for effective performance appraisal. In many schools today, the principal (perhaps with one or two assistants) is expected somehow to work closely enough with his dozens or even hundreds of subordinates to effectively evaluate their individual performance. This is a simple delusion.

Many teachers have their performance rated by a person who directly observes their performance in the classroom for perhaps a total of an hour or two in the entire school year. Worse, meaningful discussions with individual teachers about performance and career development are infrequent, if not rare. In fact, some principals only infrequently roam the halls and "look in" on the classrooms to see how things are going.

Further, it is not unusual for a teacher to have advance notice of an observation session, which allows a lackluster teacher to prepare a much better than average, though non-representative, showing. Supervisors in these circumstances are in no position to conduct an effective performance appraisal. Indeed, many teachers have jobs without any meaningful supervision at all.

In contrast, the master teacher concept calls for a small group of teachers to work closely together as a team under the direct supervision of a master teacher. This close working relationship would provide much more opportunity for the supervisor to ascertain a teacher's performance than would ever be possible in the traditional setting.

In addition to providing subordinates with daily feedback on performance and also regular dialogue about educational concerns, a supervisor should conduct two carefully planned and executed annual performance appraisal discussions with each subordinate, perhaps at the conclusion of each semester.

The formal appraisal discussion should address specific individual and team goals and objectives, the supervisor/subordinate relationship, the teacher's instructional performance and performance criteria, and the career developmental needs and interests of the teacher. Additionally, the master teacher is in a position of leadership for a team and in this discussion is subject to constructive criticism from the subordinate. The overall appraisal results, then, determine how much of the maximum one-third will apply to the teacher's raise.

Short of implementing a master teacher organization, the school system administration should at the least strongly encourage principals and other supervisory administrators to maintain a daily presence in every hallway and in every classroom. If only it would happen often enough, an administrator's visit to a classroom would at worst be barely noticed and at best welcomed as another opportunity to engage him in dialogue about the subject at hand; the administrator should be viewed by teacher and student alike as another member of the school system team rather than as a threatening, outside figure of authority.

Be assured that I do not make this recommendation without much consideration. Indeed, the issue of "merit pay" developed in my experience as a teacher years ago. At the time, I was quite opposed to the idea. What concerned me was the fact that my entire raise would depend upon the opinion of a single person who rarely observed my performance and who seldom interacted in a meaningful way with me and my associates on instructional matters.

In such a scenario, incompetent teachers can be rewarded and excellent teachers punished even more so than by the conventional, motivation-numbing salary schedule. My recommendation, by contrast, is aimed at increasing the likelihood of an effective performance appraisal process, at encouraging team-building within teams and across the system, and at providing teachers with career growth and development opportunities that give tangible recognition for excellence.

Obviously, I am not providing detail regarding performance criteria (although I have definitive thoughts about this), salary amounts, the mechanics involved with promotional steps, and the like. Instead, my intent is to offer a philosophical base upon which professionals and administrators can build a salary program that is tied to individual performance, team-building, and career growth and development opportunities for professional employees.

Last, it is the school administrators who are as much in need of effective performance management as the professional staff, and the responsibility for the *oversight* of this must rest with the school board.

Chapter 3

From Technicians to Professionals

What chef wants to cook in a fast-food restaurant?

A long time ago, teachers had more authority than they do today in determining curriculum, instructional methods, and classroom management. Indeed, they were professionals and highly respected by society.

By contrast, we now have sizable bureaucracies as obstacles to innovation and responsiveness in education. Government is too mired in political agendas to allow needed changes to proceed. Large publishers are too far removed from the front lines of education, too close to the profit motive, and too driven by demands for the standardization of curriculum materials to develop effective, flexible instructional materials.

And school systems, like bureaucracies, tend toward centralization, standardization, and a rigid organizational and procedural style of operation. Essentially, teachers are totally controlled by these larger entities. Accordingly, they have been robbed of their professionalism.

An analogy with the restaurant industry comes to mind. On the one hand, you have a fine restaurant. A chef has great expertise and great authority in the kitchen. The raw materials are top quality and expensive. The menu is varied and tailored to meet the demands of clients. Indeed, meeting the wants and needs of each customer is of paramount importance, such that intelligent responsiveness to clients is a norm. The meal is consumed in a pleasant, unhurried environment.

On the other hand, consider the typical fast-food restaurant. The cooks are required to follow simple, highly standardized procedures, such that little skill is involved. Autonomy is subordinated to " the system." The raw materials are of minimal quality and as inexpensive as can be gotten away with. The menu is simple; exceptions and special arrangements are not easily accommodated, if at all. The whole operation is geared to a low-cost, high volume, standardized process for maximum "efficiency." Indeed, the wants and needs of individuals are subordinated to satisfying the most basic, hurried cravings of the masses.

Akin to the fast-food cook, many teachers have been reduced to *classroom technicians* (not to be confused with the "education technicians" described in Chapter 1). There are too many classes in which the content is completely dictated by the textbook and its associated materials. Prefabricated tests, quizzes and work sheets are simply photocopied en masse. The content, procedural directions, and testing methodology are thus standardized and leave little room for variance.

Teachers today are required to call upon their own skills of creativity and inquiry stimulation to a much smaller degree than in years past. Students tend to be herded through the system; and while there is a lot of talk about "individualization," there is not much opportunity for this in a class of 25 or 30 youngsters.

Given the large numbers of students to be managed in a classroom and given the emphasis on the standardization of content via the textbook and/or a state-mandated curriculum, most teachers today find it very difficult (if not impossible) to be sensitive to and responsive to the unique qualities and needs of individual students and class groups. There is constant pressure on the teacher to "go with the program," cover the prescribed content, and attempt to manage the behavior of a large group of youngsters.

The level of judgment our better teachers are called on to exercise comes nowhere close to their capabilities. Decisions of any consequence are made at higher levels. In fact, teachers tend not to be asked for opinions or input on substantive educational issues at all. And even when they are asked, it too often amounts to an empty, for-show exercise.

While this is a source of great frustration for teachers who would prefer to be treated as professionals, it is ironically a blessing for those teachers who lack the skills or the intrinsic motivation to be anything more than education technicians. Lackluster and incompetent teachers like things just as they are, thank you.

Whether by choice or not, many teachers have been reduced to classroom technicians, many of whom:

- try to "cover" the prescribed content for the class as dictated by the established curriculum and textbook — no more, no less;
- tend to rely heavily on prefabricated tests, quizzes, work sheets, and audiovisuals;
- lack the time (while some lack the skills or the motivation) to discern the students' level of *understanding* of the most basic concepts and terms used in daily classroom activities;
- must follow all the standardized rules and procedures (listing behavioral objectives in a certain way in the classroom each day, having a certain number of grades in the grade book, etc.);

- are uncomfortable exercising judgment in varying from established rules/procedures, even though to do so would provide a better outcome in a particular situation;
- would be intimidated by having to develop supplementary learning experiences from scratch;
- may be really nice people and love children but who simply lack the skills to motivate and challenge students to perform to their potential;
- are comfortable with the status quo and averse to changes in procedures, schedules, academic content, teaching methods, and so on;
- more highly value controlled classroom behavior and activities than the occurrence of substantive learning (the room may be quiet—with students "paying attention" — while little learning is taking place);
- would generally be uncomfortable if called upon to participate in a dialogue with the purpose of developing improvements in educational programs;
- are unlikely to question or challenge "the system", the administration, or peers, *even when the best interests of the children are at stake*;
- lack the ability or motivation to cultivate in children the skills of reasoning, critical thinking, analysis, and creative problem-solving;
- view the job as limited to the classroom and seldom devote much time at home and in the community developing *original* plans, materials, test questions, and the like;
- tend to provide passively received instruction, as opposed to interactively *engaging* the students in the subject matter and requiring them to think;
- have lost the enthusiasm that may have existed at an earlier time; may gripe about problems with select peers but never do anything constructive to improve things or resolve problems.

When it comes to the professionalism of its staff, the single, most important improvement needed in most school systems is to implement an effective performance management program. Ideally, this would incorporate the master teacher organizational structure and the compensation ideas in my earlier writing. Even without these changes, however, improvements could easily and inexpensively be made in how teachers are treated and in the quality of their performance management.

First, consider this notion: A starting place to help teachers to become more professional is to treat them as professionals. In its simplest terms I believe that professionalism encompasses high levels of expertise, authority, autonomy, respectability, ethical standards, sound judgment, and accountability.

Perhaps to a greater extent than with the other elements of professionalism, authority and autonomy distinguish the professional from the technician.

Ask yourself whether the following list of job attributes describes the job of a "professional":

- the employee is required to sign-in each morning to show proper arrival time;
- the employee is seldom included in decision-making sessions about substantive issues related to the job;
- supervisory expectations are limited to covering the day-to-day routine while controlling any problems that arise—as opposed to strategic considerations;
- little time and incentive are available for research and the development of improved performance strategies;
- everything is systematized, including every moment of the employee's day and even the use of office equipment and other resources;
- meetings are tightly controlled by an authoritarian with a specific agenda; information is normally received passively

by employees; there is seldom any meaningful dialogue about problem areas and substantive issues;

- the creative, brainstorming, problem-solving talents of the employee go largely unchallenged, untapped, and neglected;
- too much of the activity in the employee's work place is done for appearances because "it's always been done that way" or as a mechanical, thoughtless, unquestioned procedure;
- rather than anticipate/prevent and talk openly about problems and improvement needs, the work place is more normally characterized as reactionary to problems in a damage-control mode; there is much reticence on all sides when it comes to direct, effective communication about problems;
- the employee often feels helpless, unsupported, and powerless to effect change.

The number of jobs in which individuals enjoy *complete* satisfaction as professionals by my definition is no doubt small. At the same time, however, I believe that teachers tend not to be treated as professionals, and this is reflected in their behavior. Here again is an inexpensive opportunity for constructive change.

The performance management of teachers, then, begins with fundamental, professional treatment. Secondly, teachers should have a compensation program that rewards professional performance with a professional-level salary and benefits package. Yes, this would constitute a major expense item in most school systems; but this important goal should be striven for, if incrementally, over several years.

The matter of compensation provides another opportunity, however, for constructive change without great expense. The compensation program should be structured to provide incentives for excellent individual performance on the job, for excellent group or team performance, and for excellent system-wide performance, as described in my writing in Chapter 2. The "salary scales" in most school systems today provide absolutely no inducement for excellent performance.

A third area of performance management in need of improvement in many school systems is the supervision of performance. It is often the case that a single person is held responsible for the performance of dozens of professional employees. The natural result is that many teachers rarely, if ever, receive meaningful supervision. My notion of effective "supervision" includes the following:

- Each teacher should participate in two comprehensive performance and development discussions each year. These should be carefully planned-for, two-way discussions as described in Chapter 2. If a teacher's performance is in need of improvement, an action plan should be mutually developed and agreed to for a probationary period to last no longer than the end of the following school year. If performance remains unsatisfactory, the teacher should be terminated. This is not to neglect the developmental portion of the discussion. Attention should also be given to training, education and other activities that will support the teacher's career interests and development.

- Each teacher's classroom should be visited/observed on a random basis frequently. Visits should take place at least once each day. It should happen often enough that it is barely noticed, except when the supervisor has something to contribute to the class.

- Supervisors should look for opportunities to talk with teachers on an informal basis about how things are going. Many problems can be identified in this way and addressed at an early stage. Too, teachers will realize that supervisors really do care about their problems.

-

- Supervisors should give frequent feedback to teachers as to their performance. If performance is strong, it should be recognized. If it needs improvement, prompt coaching should be provided.
- A supervisor should act as and be viewed as a coach, a guide, a supporter, a facilitator, a cooperative trouble-shooter, a resource, a team-builder, a source of enthusiasm and vision, and yes: a supervisor of effective performance.

Supervisors should conduct meetings with individuals and with groups in a way which encourages ideas and opinions. Candor should be viewed as an essential problem-solving tool. Professionals in a meeting need to feel that their views make an important contribution. Accordingly, a teacher who contributed an idea, question, or concern should receive meaningful feedback and inclusion at the earliest opportunity. Decisions should often be made on a consensus basis.

Some of these supervisory traits would require only a change in supervisory style, while others require increased supervisory availability. Short of the organizational change enumerated in Chapter 1, a school system could apportion the duties of its administrative personnel so as to satisfy the supervisory load required by a truly effective program of supervision.

The fourth area of performance management worth emphasis is that of training and development. It is partly here that the development and the performance improvement portions of the performance and development discussion are put into action. Supervisor and subordinate alike should be on the lookout for speakers, workshops, seminars, literature, training and educational opportunities that will enhance progress toward individual, team and system objectives.

In summary, too many excellent teachers will continue to be frustrated, too many lackluster teachers will continue to be lackluster, and too many incompetent teachers will continue doing damage in the classroom until they are treated as professionals, given the resources and support to perform well, and provided expectations and require-ments for performance which are at the least, satisfactory.

Chapter 4

Professional Responsibility

If you are not part of the solution, you are part of the problem.

Many years ago, I heard a school board member comment that "the only time we ever hear anything from the teachers is at salary time." The truth of the statement prevented me from taking umbrage. And if it is true that administrators have been negligent in earnestly soliciting input from teachers on educational matters, it is also true that teachers have not done an effective job of asserting their concerns and recommendations to administrators.

Despite the illogic of it, there is nonetheless a tremendous communication gap between teachers at the front lines of education and administrators who determine policy and procedures. As long as this gap continues, progress toward excellence will be retarded and our children will continue as victims of adult ineptness.

Just the notion that there exists a "teacher union" on the one side and the school administration on the other presents implications beyond a communication gap. The need for "negotiation" to achieve agreement on important issues and a lack of trust on both sides result in inefficiencies in how the whole system works. One is left to wonder at the great potential for real progress toward excellence which rests untapped because we are not pulling in the same direction. Too much of our energy is diverted away from the children.

One could study most school systems carefully and discover across the professional ranks an alarming lack of cooperation and good will; feelings of isolation, self-centeredness and defensiveness; racial intolerance and unfriendliness (and the children are watching); we-they attitudes; lowered morale; tremendous frustration (on the part of caring teachers); and apathy (on the part of lackluster and incompetent teachers).

This all begs the question: What does the leadership of the local professional teachers' association do to develop programs aimed at improving the competence and professionalism of its members, to help their membership cope with stress and frustration, to break down the communication barriers that exist across and between every level of the school system organization, and to take positions on important educational issues and place recommendations before the school administration?

What must the image of the "professional association" be when the public perception of its activities is limited to a fight once a year for higher salaries and the threat of a defense against the firing of an incompetent teacher?

My recommendation is that the professional association make an assessment of its roles in meeting the professional needs of its members individually and as a group (this would include counseling unhappy and lackluster teachers and withholding support from incompetent teachers), in addressing the educational interests of children, and as an agent for change in helping the overall school system to work better.

Members should be organized into groups and tasked with developing specific goals and objectives to include follow-up activities and progress reporting. This effort should be characterized by effective communications, a positive mindset, and a high value placed on teamwork across the system, especially as this relates to working *with* the school system administration; we must close the gap.

This should place the association (or union) in a position to appear regularly before the school system administration and/or school board with observations and recommendations, as well as offers to co-operate and help to make improvements.

Our children are our most important resource. Providing a quality education is of paramount importance. With the foregoing, who would disagree? But we must guard against merely giving lip service to this, and we must be vigilant against allowing the day-to-day travails of managing our own school system, our own school, or our own classroom to cause us to lose sight of why we are here.

It seems to me the maxim applies well: *If you are not part of the solution, you are part of the problem.* I challenge the professional ranks in education to share proactively in the responsibility for progress toward excellence.

Chapter 5

Meaningful Attention Versus Mass Production

Rollin', rollin', rollin'... Keep them doggies rollin'!

To put some perspective on the issue of classroom size, consider the extremes: At the first extreme you will find the Socratic tutor in a one-on-one relationship with the student. This extreme provides a highly effective instructional/learning environment with "individualization" at its best. However, social interactions with peers are nonexistent, and for most parents today this approach would be cost-prohibitive.

At the other extreme, the teacher-pupil ratio is enormous. While individual attention is impossible, large masses of students can be efficiently herded through this process at minimal cost.

But there is more to this issue than a balance between individual attention and cost per pupil. The nature of the students must also be examined, and this includes their age and maturity and also the values and motivation they bring with them into the classroom. Thus, having

150 motivated students in a single college classroom may provide an acceptable learning environment at a very low cost.

Let us turn now to the typical American classroom (grades K-12). In most of them you will find a broad mix of qualities across the students in the room: the respectful and the disrespectful, the intelligent and the learning disabled, the emotionally mature and the emotionally and mentally challenged, the confident and the insecure, and the loud and the quiet. Some are rude, some are full of hate, and some are full of sadness. Some want to learn, while others could not care less (no matter *what* the teacher does).

You will find students who are self-disciplined and others who are not. The rebellious are there, full of contempt, along with others who appreciate decency. There are the healthy and the wise, and there are drug abusers and pushers. There are teens out of wedlock who proudly flaunt their pregnancy while others conceal this and give birth alone. Some are rich, some poor. Some emit repulsive body odor. Some delight in distracting others, disrupting the class and giving the teacher a hard time. Some come from a supportive, nurturing background and a home in which such things as reading, working, cooperation and learning are valued; and others come from an entirely different background. Some are gracious and appreciative while others are simply spoiled brats. There is no such thing as the "average student."

Now, just for a moment, I ask that you picture yourself standing before a class of, say, 31 such students as their teacher. You are fully responsible not only for the group of them (this is your responsibility for effective "classroom management") but also for each one of them, for you are responsible for each child's learning progress.

I believe that I could write another book, drawing upon my own experience, describing the daily challenges you would face with this group. Even if you were to read such a book, I say to you that unless you were to have this experience for yourself, you cannot imagine how stressful and how exhausting it can be to control the behavior of the group, to motivate each student, to prepare interesting instruction, and to measure the learning progress of each student.

The relative merits of homogeneous versus heterogeneous grouping are not the issue. The issue is the teacher-pupil ratio, and here is the simple truth: Probably following a geometric curve, the fewer students a teacher has in a given classroom, the more depth of instruction is possible; the more manageable the behavior of the group becomes; the more individual attention can be given; the more opportunity there will be for each student to develop the learning and satisfaction that comes from classroom participation; the more time the teacher will have for innovative lesson planning; and the better job the teacher will be able to do in evaluating the academic progress of each student.

My view of the relationship between teacher-student ratio and instructional effectiveness is categorized as follows:

- One to ten students in the class: Insufficient instructional benefit is gained in this ratio range to justify the increased expense, which is cost-prohibitive anyway.

- Fifteen to eighteen students in the class: This ratio is needed in all language arts and English classes to provide sufficient individual attention in these most critical of academic classes; this ratio would also allow additional, precious time to the teacher for the exceptionally heavy workload involved with instructional planning and student performance evaluation.

- Eighteen to twenty-two students in the class: This constitutes a good ratio for most other classes.

- Twenty-five to thirty students in the class: In this range, the class has taken on a mass identity. Trouble-makers find it easier to distract others in the larger group setting. While good teachers can still effectively manage a class of this size, an appreciable decline in instructional quality has taken place.

- Thirty-two to thirty-eight students in the class: The ability of the teacher to give instructional attention to individual students gives way in this range to a concern for effectively managing or controlling the students as a group. Worse, there is a natural pressure to focus academic attention on the middle bulk of the class; the brightest and the slowest in the class are left out as the teacher has less time for individualization.

Depending somewhat on the subject, the sheer volume of paperwork involved is exerting great pressure on the teacher to "cut corners" with instructional planning, class activities, and student evaluation. Those teachers who insist on quality despite this pressure spend up to two and three hours per night trying to get the job done (with no "overtime pay" involved).

Given that a lower teacher-pupil ratio provides a better quality education but is more costly, it is regrettable that many people color the dilemma with such questions as "How much can we afford?" But framing the issue in this way only leads us to the notion that all that is needed is to determine "what the budget can allow" and then let the teacher-pupil ratio fall into place accordingly; and this is the wrong mindset.

The more apt question is "How highly do we value education?"

Certainly, I realize there is a natural resistance to increasing taxes, for this is a highly charged political and emotional kind of issue. I wonder, however, how much the general population really knows about the problems, needs, and opportunities involved with education. My bet is that most people have little understanding about why our nation's public education systems are producing a relatively weak product.

The public should be educated about the school system's needs for increased funding. The public should be helped to understand why, by example, a reduced teacher-pupil ratio is important for our children's sake. Why shouldn't the school system actively market this, as well as other causes of education? If this results in a battle for money, then why not engage the enemy? Which side has the long view and the worthy cause?

While it may be unrealistic for a school system to dramatically improve its teacher-pupil ratio across the system within a year, it seems to me that small battles could be waged as opportunities arise. The subject areas and grades in greatest need could be improved first, with others following over a few years' time.

Educational issues like the teacher-pupil ratio should not automatically take a back seat year after year to budgetary constraints—not without serious argument.

Chapter 6

What Did You Expect?

We are not as powerful as we used to be because over the past three decades, the Asian values of our parents' generation—work hard, study, save, invest, live within your means—have given way to subprime values...

—Thomas Friedman, columnist with *The New York Times*, and published in *The Virginian-Pilot* 5-6-2008

While it may be naïve or an oversimplification, it seems to me that my generation and especially my parents' generation were the recipients of high expectations for performance, whether at home, at school, or in the public eye. There was work to do and value was placed on doing a good job. It was considered important to make a contribution, to do your part, and to cooperate in a group effort. As we matured, this translated into our placing expectations upon ourselves—let's call that "taking responsibility" for our own actions and inactions. Whither did that go?

Regardless, these were *learned* attributes, taught to us by our "elders"—our elders at home, in church, and at school. Good work and good behavior were simply expected. And they were produced, "or else," meaning that there were consequences for our actions and our inactions. Sure, there was goofing-off, rudeness (probably not much of that...) and laziness, but if an objective comparison were to be made between generations, the stark contrast would be obvious.

It has been argued that youths have just changed and the schools have to adjust. This disgusting notion acts to worsen the problem, and it demonstrates that the fault truly lies not with our youths but rather with our current generation of elders—you and me—for our acquiescence to mediocrity and our refusal to accept responsibility for the sad state of education being provided to our youths.

We blame Congress, we blame other parents, we blame "kids these days," and so on. And then we ask "but what can *I* do?" If we cannot think of anything, then we are in big trouble indeed. The foundational question, then, focuses on the expectations we place on *ourselves*, not only to effect change but as an example to our youths, who see everything we do and do not do. They know where our values are, and they are excellent learners, no matter what their grades in school may suggest.

Let us turn to the place of expectations as applied within the schools, realizing now that an effective use of expectations within the school itself will be handicapped without resonance and an active involvement on the part of every element of the community.

It did not take long in my teaching experience for me to notice that youngsters tended to perform just about to the level I expected them to, both behaviorally and academically. I saw teachers who required little of their students, with the result that their students exerted little effort to perform well. And there were other teachers who were very specific in defining high expectations for their students and in following through with them each day of the school year. Interestingly, the teachers who were best at this were not viewed as "mean"; to the contrary, they tended to be highly respected by their students.

In my view, there are many classrooms across our nation in which the students are simply not required to perform up to their potential, and this is a major factor in the lackluster performance of our youths. For the most part, the reasons for low expectations in the classroom are threefold: (1) the teacher is a poor performer and unable to convey and/or administer high expectations; (2) there is a lack of training available to teachers on this subject, and there is no "sense of mission" about high expectations promulgated by the school system; and (3) some teachers, after years of daily battle with little or no support, feel worn-out, overwhelmed, and disheartened — these are the capable teachers who as a survival strategy have lowered their expectations of student performance.

Certainly, there are teachers in every system who expect and stimulate high academic and behavioral performance on the part of their students in the face of constant pressure to do otherwise. Maintaining high expectations in the classroom, I assure you, is extremely challenging, exhausting, hard work — every day. In my view, teachers who do well with this are in a minority in most school systems.

Another number of teachers provide a barely acceptable climate of expectations. And still another group lacks the ability and/or motivation to implement meaningful expectations to any degree; ironically, some of these teachers are viewed as "strict" by their students.

This is to suggest that the successful implementation of high expectations is much more than a simple matter of authoritarian control or strictness with students. Rather, success with high expectations depends upon success with other elements of the teacher-student relationship, such as trust, respect, fairness, firmness, sincerity, and effective communications.

The following occurs to me as a skeleton guide for a teacher in implementing a program of high expectations with students. Each teacher should

- place upon students expectations which will challenge and develop their abilities to reason, to communicate effectively, and to apply their learning skills. This will mean work for the students in developing, as examples, their skills of note making, class participation, concept development, grammar, speech, inquiry and spelling;

- place upon students expectations which will provide an effective climate for learning within the classroom setting. Old-fashioned "paying attention" and respect for whoever has the floor are examples of essential classroom conduct;

- be clear and complete in specifying in advance what students can expect of the teacher in terms of the instructional process, the testing and evaluation process, the type of relationship (mutual trust and respect) to be established, and the course content and types of activities that will be utilized;

- take time to enter a dialogue with students in considering the reasoning behind high expectations. Students need to know, by example, why and how the development of good communicative skills is essential to their future success and happiness;

- be clear and complete in explaining and documenting in advance what the consequences will be for appropriate and inappropriate classroom behavior and academic performance. As examples, students should know up-front how much spelling will count on the essay questions in geography, and they need to know up-front exactly what the consequences will be for disruptive classroom behavior.

No less important and much more challenging than specifying up-front expectations will be the teacher's daily follow-through in reminding, encouraging, and requiring compliance with established expectations. Indeed, this is the most demanding, energy-sapping element of a teacher's day-to-day classroom responsibilities. But without this, students have no stimulus and no framework within which to grow and develop their maturity and their academic performance.

The development or rekindling of a program of high expectations should become an important school system objective with results that flow into every classroom uniformly. Every teacher who fails to insist on the best performance from students is stealing away some of their future success and happiness. The school system leadership has an important responsibility to ensure that a program of high expectations becomes a *mindset* across the entire system.

So, we must raise the expectations for academic and behavioral performance on the part of our students. That is an easy decision as we prepare for dinner and the evening news. Must we not first raise the expectations for our school *systems* (not just the teachers)? But hold! How can any such expectations be raised unless we as individual members of the community initiate the process? And we can only accomplish this by first learning more about the school environment ourselves and by then speaking out about what we believe are the needs for change.

Chapter 7

A Real Teacher

Education is not the filling of a pail,
but the lighting of a fire.

—William Butler Yeats

L ighting fires properly is quite difficult, consumes significant resources, and requires extraordinary talent in a specially prepared
environment. Filling pails is another matter, however, even if we use
an impressive-looking liquid concocted by higher authorities, remote
experts, and other entities with something to gain from the success of
the enterprise.

Indeed, we have been perfecting our pail-filling procedures and
have only to walk into any classroom to see the prefabricated objectives
for such procedures clearly stated in behavioral terms on the board at
the start of each day, there being penalties for the teacher if there is any
deviation. This, without regard to whether substantive learning takes
place that day.

As if igniting too few flames were not enough, we have come to
demand that our little pails be filled in a uniform way with a highly
standardized and controlled volume, regardless of the size of the pails
involved. To maximize our efficiencies, we have adjusted the volume
and the procedures we use to accommodate the highest possible but
lowest common denominator of pail capacity.

While the larger pails are essentially left on their own to obtain a fill-up, the system results can be made to look good even though they address the lowest common denominator of pail capacity and even though we are still only talking about filling pails. See how easy it is to forget about an education firestorm?

We are getting really good at this—finally, something we are successfully using on a massive scale to address our education woes. It is cost-effective, easy to train the less-able to conduct, easy to measure results, easy to hold teachers accountable based on uniformly dictated criteria, and easy to use statistics to show "improvement." What more could a school official or politician want? Unfortunately, the pails we are filling are winding up being used as fire buckets.

The Washington Times columnist Suzanne Fields wrote in an editorial titled "Rising Tide of Ignorance" in the May 12, 2008 edition of *The Virginian Pilot*:

> No Child Left Behind legislation was well intentioned, but its emphasis on testing has had unintended consequences. Not only do many teachers teach to the test, but literature and history have been moved to the margins, preserving ignorance and shorting subjects that emphasize creative and critical thinking.

How many fires can we light by teaching to the test? And how many teachers with a passion to stimulate expansive thinking and substantive learning are being stifled by oppressively standardized procedures and limited curriculums?

The effectiveness of a teacher is determined by two very different elements, almost akin to the old environment-versus-genetics mix. On the "environment" side, you have the autonomy, encouragement, support, tools, guidelines, and facilities that are provided to the teacher by the system—or not. On the "genetics" side, you have the character, motivation, skills, knowledge, and values that the teacher brings into the classroom—or not.

It is important to distinguish between these two elements because as surely as you could have an unmotivated teacher performing poorly in the classroom despite a great work environment, so also you can have a great teacher whose effectiveness is squashed to whatever extent by an oppressive work environment. While the former is readily addressed in a strong school, the latter prevails to an alarming extent all across the nation and has been impervious to change. No wonder we are avoidably losing our best teachers and experiencing difficulty attracting excellent candidates to the profession.

Having distinguished between the two, let us set aside the environmental element now in order to better focus on the "genetics" of a real teacher.

More than textbooks, a new building, teacher aides, A/V materials, air conditioning, and a specific curriculum, it is the quality of the classroom teacher that determines the effectiveness of the instructional program. *If you do not have a quality teacher in the classroom, all the rest makes no difference.*

While for the lackluster teacher the job is relatively easy, for the excellent teacher it is one of the most challenging, demanding, stressful and exhausting jobs to be found anywhere. The combination of qualities that make for an excellent teacher includes some very unique characteristics and sets this job quite apart from the more typical types of work which require a narrower field of skills and attributes. Considering this, good teachers should be sought out and nurtured, and excellent teachers should be treasured as an immensely valuable asset.

What follow are what I consider to be the requisite characteristics of a quality teacher. I have organized them into four categories. Those in "A" relate to the disposition of the teacher and seem to me to be intrinsic; those in "B" describe qualities that will determine the teacher/child relationship; those in "C" are more traditionally thought of as the "job-related" qualities to look for, but in my view they must extend far beyond a nice personality, good posture and content knowledge; "D" does not occur to most people as important.

These categories are not in a priority order, and I consider every single characteristic to be important; the excellent teacher must "have it all":

A1. ENTHUSIASM! — a contagious quality, essential to motivation in children. It empowers the curriculum by energizing a child's interest. It fosters the development of a positive outlook, commitment, and team effort. If the teacher is without this, the classroom will have a lifeless, even suppressive pall about it, particularly for those students who are most capable.

A2. A LOVE FOR CHILDREN AND FOR TEACHING, for tapping into a child's energy and for *stimulating wonder and a thirst for learning*. This is an important area of satisfaction for the excellent teacher. It is a driving force for excellent instruction, and our children are the beneficiaries. Lacking this, a teacher is holding the job for the wrong reasons.

A3. AN ABIDING CONCERN ABOUT CHILDREN, their future, and society. The best teachers view children as our nation's most valuable resource, and they treat them accordingly. Lackluster teachers give lip service to this, but they really do not care that much about it. This is the other main driving force for excellent instruction, and it is this quality which causes the best teachers to become terribly frustrated when they see politics, ignorance, or incompetence stand in the way of improvements or even "doing things right" on a day-to-day basis in education.

A4. HIGH VALUE ON INSTILLING LEARNING TOOLS and resourcefulness in our children. Among the most important (and challenging) tasks before a teacher is that of helping a child learn how to learn and how to be resourceful. The learning skills (HOW TO listen, inquire, use resources, plan, experiment, innovate, gather and analyze information, form hypotheses, infer, deduce, make effective communications, and make decisions) are in my view increasingly important in our age of rapid change and quickly outdated knowledge. How can we hope for improvements in our society without young people who know how to think critically and solve problems? Yet, too many teachers do not value this responsibility and choose instead the much easier job of "imparting knowledge" or adhering strictly to a standardized curriculum. That a school system would tolerate such content-limited instruction in even one classroom seems to me irresponsible.

B1. RESPONSIVENESS TO CHILDREN. The best teachers (1) thirst for students' questions, for they realize that the best kind of learning takes place upon the child's initiative, such that *inquiry is encouraged*—even insisted upon; (2) care about the concerns of children, for this is the most fertile ground for learning, even if the result is to stray for a few moments away from the lesson plan or the content limitations of the textbook; and (3) are not intimidated by not having all the answers for students' questions; rather, the best teachers know how to guide a student's quest to a satisfying end. This almost subversive tactic makes the child's learning process even more meaningful. Unbelievably, in every system there are unresponsive teachers who suppress inquiry, however subtly; the tragic result is children who have learned not to ask questions and who resent the hypocrisy of the educational institution.

B2. HIGH EXPECTATIONS OF CHILDREN, both academically and behaviorally. In my experience, students normally perform up to the expectations of the teacher. When a teacher is reasonable, "up-front," and clear in presenting high expectations, the students will perform accordingly. Superficially, they may gripe about this, but deep down they desire and need it; natural outcomes beyond performance include feelings of pride and security.

On a related note, teachers must take special steps to instill a SENSE OF RESPONSIBILITY in our children with regard to their behavior at all times, whether the issue is a term paper, a science fair project, test results, disruptive behavior, drug abuse, littering, homework, or something that just needs doing. If we fail to expect our children to be responsible for themselves, it will not happen, and we adults are the ones to blame. I can assure you that the follow-through on this item presents a daily, exhausting challenge to our best teachers, for there is resistance from every quarter and no reward for the large effort involved.

B3. <u>FIRM, FAIR AND FRIENDLY</u> presence in the classroom. The inseparable partner to high academic and behavioral expectations is a combination of firmness in enforcement (the teacher must have resolve) and fairness and continuity in both design and application. A teacher's failure to provide **both** firmness and fairness is an open invitation for disrespect. Too, a classroom teacher without a friendly demeanor is depriving children of a valuable, life-enriching role model quality. A teacher should be able to laugh with the students and to laugh at himself; a quality teacher is unafraid of being human before his students.

B4. <u>SINCERITY.</u> This quality in a teacher expands far beyond a nice personality trait. The best teachers are strong in this quality, and there is no hiding the having of it (or the absence of it) from even younger students. This trait empowers everything else in the "B" category, and it reveals the truth of everything in the "A" category on the part of the teacher who possesses it. The sincere teacher takes his job very seriously, and children recognize this. The sincere teacher takes the children very seriously, and children appreciate this. The sincere teacher abhors pretentiousness. The sincere teacher means what he says in the classroom, and the children know it. SINCERITY BREEDS RESPECT. To the extent sincerity is lacking, disrespect will fill the void.

C1. INTELLIGENCE AND ACQUIRED SKILLS. There are many forms of intelligence. Certain ones of them, along with certain acquired skills, contribute to the excellent teacher's abilities to (1) have a reasonable command of the subject matter; (2) analyze situations effectively, recognize and solve problems, and learn from mistakes; (3) be innovative and creative; (4) keep abreast of new ideas and knowledge; (5) tap resources effectively; (6) stimulate, challenge and make progress with all learners, from the slowest to the fastest; and (7) provide a dynamic classroom environment and keep several steps ahead of the students—this requires a sharp wit and effective planning.

C2. PROFESSIONALISM. There is much more to being a professional than having a degree, more than being a subject-matter expert, more than knowing how to copy behaviorally stated learning objectives out of a guide into a lesson plan book, and more than having "the look" of a professional (poise, neat dress, bearing). The most important attributes of a teacher as a professional, it seems to me, are as follows: (1) all of the "A," "B," and "C" qualities stated heretofore; (2) a high level of intrinsic motivation, which translates into a sense of responsibility, initiative and drive; (3) high ethical standards (the true professional is a highly principled individual); (4) performance with a constant focus on the best interests of the children and a dedication to improving the educational process; (5) a team-player posture with respect to other professionals and administrators; (6) excellent communicative and interpersonal skills; and (7) an even temperament.

D1. <u>RESILIENCE</u>. In order for a teacher to continue to work at a professional level and to enjoy this career over time, he must be resilient. Without this, the caring teacher will soon become unhappy and frustrated — even depressed — or else lower his expectations, sacrifice his professionalism, and just coast; and to whatever extent the teacher makes a "happy medium" adjustment between quality and incompetence, the children lose out. For the truth is that while lackluster teachers enjoy a fairly easy job, the best teachers regularly face a very heavy workload (extending into the home) along with tremendous stress and frustration associated with this job. It is important that teachers develop and receive tools to help alleviate pressures due to workload and stress.

It occurs to me that one might see an unreasonable degree of idealism in my notion about the composition of a quality classroom teacher. Certainly, I can appreciate the fact that we are all human beings, each with our own set of strengths and frailties. I submit, however, that the human race is fully capable of generating an ample supply of teachers who fall within a good to outstanding range with each of the stated qualities.

To take the position that such quality across the entire teaching staff is unrealistic and unattainable is to acquiesce to mediocrity in our schools. To take the position that "We already have an excellent staff and excellent instruction" is to practice denial in the face of quietly suffering students and caring teachers. Even one lackluster teacher is too many; and to allow even one incompetent teacher to continue doing damage in the classroom is reprehensible.

It is incumbent upon both the school administration and the professional group to address the needs for quality personnel and instruction. Careful attention must be given to the recruitment, selection, organization, performance management, development, and retention of quality personnel across the system.

And as many members of the business community have, school systems should seek out professional guidance and training to manage the difficult process of change from an industrial-age, top-down, bureaucratic environment to one which nourishes the real teacher and spawns the flames of learning among our young.

Chapter 8

Teach Them How to Learn

What is the difference between violet and purple?

The normal response in the adult community is, "Who cares?"
No wonder our children are receiving an inadequate education.
They learn best by our example.

Most students in my experience were highly reluctant to employ a thoughtful or analytical process with their class work, whatever the subject. They would have been happy if I had required them to memorize vocabulary definitions and if I had asked them the same questions in the same way as those already in their experience. I remember that it was a "constant battle," particularly in the first part of the year, to get them to wonder, to question, to figure something out, to apply what they know in a new way or in a different set of circumstances—indeed, to think.

There are many powerful forces aligned against a substantive learning process, not the least of which is the students' natural tendency to avoid what they perceive to be work. I do not fault the children for this, however, believing that an important part of a teacher's responsibility is to overcome this resistance with the use of high expectations and motivational methods of instruction.

Other forces over which teachers have very little control combine to detract from meaningful learning in the classroom. These include high teacher-pupil ratios, parental noninvolvement, inadequate school-wide expectations of student academic and behavioral performance, and an oppressive volume of paperwork and inefficient procedures. A subtle but important resulting symptom can be found in too many classrooms in which the focus is overwhelmingly on the objective over the subjective in classroom activities as well as in test questioning. Thus energy is further removed from real understanding and from the development of concepts and learning skills.

While lackluster teachers have little interest in this issue, competent teachers find that one of the most infuriating and saddening elements of their experience in education is the contrast between the potential of children to learn and the reality that our educational systems tend as much to hinder substantive learning as to enhance it. Certainly, there are pockets of excellence to be found, but in too many classrooms, "education" is a passive, uninspiring, even intellectually deadening enterprise.

Even if little is to be done immediately about such problems as high teacher-pupil ratios, there is an opportunity for improvement in many classrooms when it comes to the development of a curriculum and methods of instruction which emphasize skills of learning. This is not to say that skills are more important than knowledge. As a matter of emphasis, rather, classroom instruction too often amounts to a mechanical coverage of content instead of an exploration of interest; a passive reception of facts at the expense of developing the abilities to discover facts; short-term, superficial, "academic" success, while the skills needed to adapt and learn throughout life receive inadequate attention.

Administrators and classroom teachers need to work cooperatively to turn this serious problem around. Objectives should be set, training sessions and follow-up consultation should be provided, and a mindset should be established across the school system — a mindset of enthusiasm, high expectations, pluck, and dedication to a substantive learning process, the basic elements of which could be as follows:

A. Concept Development

An effective command of the English language is imperative to success. If it is claimed that we already have adequate standards of language achievement, then I submit they are not high enough by a long shot.

Certainly, the rules of grammar and spelling are vital in this effort. As important and more fundamental, however, is an understanding of the building blocks of language — words. In my view, vocabulary should be taught each week in every single class and in every single grade; even in PE, in vocational arts, in driver's ed, and in art.

The emphasis must be on concept development rather than memorized definitions, however, and this will require a dynamic instructional process in the classroom. Vocabulary testing should require students to demonstrate understanding of the meaning of a term by applying it correctly in a new way or in a different set of circumstances from what was "studied."

The content for this instruction should not be limited to the vocabulary list at the end of each chapter in the textbook. Every section in the reading materials and every dialogue which takes place in the classroom should provide opportunities for concept development.

By example, how much sense does it make for students to routinely repeat the Pledge of Allegiance when they do not understand the meaning of terms such as allegiance, republic and pledge? Astute teachers will not assume that all students understand the terms used in day-to-day classroom activities. This must be a matter of daily consciousness and attention, with new vocabulary terms being added and discussed "on the run" each day.

Furthermore, it would be well for each student's curriculum to include a study of the etymology of words and phrases. This could take the form of two units of study (of perhaps a grading period in duration) — one in middle school and one in the 10th grade or so. Or, etymology could be woven into existing Language Arts and English programs. The point here is that the depth of understanding involved for many terms will be richly enhanced when there is also understanding about their components and background.

B. An Interactive, Inquiry-Based Style of Instruction

In too many classrooms, the teacher plays the role of one who imparts knowledge to the students, while the students take a basically passive role. Students' natural inquisitiveness is constrained by the teacher's need to maintain "control" of the classroom and to remain ever-focused on the content item at hand. Some teachers simply do not have the skills which would allow the students to engage in an active learning process.

Students learn best, however, when they are motivated to learn; and the odds that they will be motivated are enhanced tremendously when they are actively involved in the process and when they feel that the outcome is something they contributed to.

The school system should provide training for its entire instructional staff in an interactive and inquiry-based style of instruction. The teacher's role should in large measure be that of a guide who encourages and rewards meaningful questioning, who seizes upon inquisitiveness and wonder as opportunities leading to satisfaction and a hunger to learn more, and who engages students in a dialogue rather than structured questions and answers. Obviously, this will require more skill and work on the part of the teacher.

There are many techniques a teacher can use to encourage inquiry and interaction. A few examples follow; but without a sincere interest in this classroom quality, the use of "techniques" will be a hollow enterprise at best — and the students will see it for what it is.

- Pertinent classroom participation should be encouraged — even rewarded.
- Teachers should frequently ask probing, follow-up questions to ensure depth of understanding, and students should be encouraged to do the same.
- In addition to making individual contributions to the class, students should be occasionally organized into teams and tasked with projects, the successful completion of which will require them to have worked cooperatively in drawing upon their individual talents.
- Teachers should make intentional errors occasionally and reward alert students who notice and offer corrections.
- Students should be actively engaged in the development of concepts by being called upon to offer what they already know, collectively.
- When something is wondered about and neither the students nor the teacher has the answers, the teacher should switch the class into an exploration mode, with activities within and outside the classroom used to discover the answers; the teacher should not adhere rigidly to the content at hand in the face of genuine interest on the part of the students in learning.

When students walk into the classroom, they should feel that this is a place in which it is perfectly normal and acceptable (for the teacher and the students alike) to not have all the answers, to ask questions, to make mistakes; to share and modify answers; to learn from everyone's mistakes; to expect and give respect to others' feelings; to draw upon all available resources to explore a line of thinking, an idea, or a task; to enjoy and value learning for its own sake. The teacher is responsible for establishing a classroom setting or "atmosphere" which promotes inquiry, interaction, and enthusiasm about learning.

C. Tools For Learning, Adaptation and Success

Memorizing facts in school serves a useful purpose. It is at least as important, however, for young people to develop tools that will enable them to accomplish tasks, resolve problems, and communicate analytically in the future — a future in which the facts will be different, the rules will be changing, and there will be an increasing dependence upon effective communications.

The "facts" I refer to include number skills, vocabulary definitions, science classifications, and even historical events, which can be subject to the whims of a publisher or the social and political climate of the day. Learning such knowledge and skills is basic to a good education, but it falls short of what our children need even now in a rapidly changing world.

Increasingly, our children need tools that will enable them to be responsive and adaptive to change without sacrificing achievement; to employ flexibility and perseverance in addressing challenging events and issues; to be thoughtful and reflective in analyzing information and in dealing with other people; and to use a logical approach in day-to-day decision-making. What follow are some tools worthy of development in our children:

A healthy mindset for change.

One has only to examine world events in government, the environment, social mores, economics/markets and science/technology to realize that change is taking place at an increasing rate. And the same is true in our homes, communities and in the workplace. Unfortunately for most of us, change is normally stressful.

Since we are unable to prevent change from occurring, it would seem wise to help children accept change as a reality, analyze trends in order to take intelligent action, look for and pursue opportunities within change, and intelligently resist change that conflicts with an individual's strong convictions or principles.

An organizational approach to tasks and problems.

Throughout life — at home, at school, in the community and in the workplace — each of us is faced with a constant stream of tasks to accomplish and problems to resolve. And too many youngsters, without guidance, do not know where to begin or how to persevere. Some of them simply quit, while for others an ineffective product is the result.

Children should be helped to develop an internal, automatic checklist of questions to refer to as they approach tasks and problems. When a youngster learns to "talk with himself" in this way, a *plan* can be laid out (even if it is a quick, mental plan) that will enhance chances for a successful outcome. Such a list may be formed as a mental buffet, with items arranged in a logical sequence to be selected from as the nature of the task or problem may warrant. Here is a sampler of such a buffet:

- Why am I doing this; is it important?
- How do I go about getting this done?
- What do I need to do first?
- What information do I need, and where can I get it?
- What resources do I need, and where can I get them?
- Whom do I need to work with on this?
- How much time will this take; do I need to budget my time?
- When does this need to be completed?
- How can I avoid unnecessary conflict or hurt feelings without sacrificing accomplishment?
- How will this person feel or react if I say it one way versus a different way?
- What can I do/say that will minimize a bad outcome and enhance the opportunity for a successful outcome?
- What obstacles are possible?
- What backup and alternatives do I need to have ready?
- Where do I need to follow-up to make sure things get done?

- Who needs to be informed, and how much information do they need?
- What outcome do I want to produce?
- How will I know that I have been successful?

As you can see, the classic who-what-where-when-why-how questions are essential in setting up a plan of action, with consideration given to resources, people, communication, time/timing, procedure and the desired product. Once the plan is set, it is a matter of execution, with the expectation that problems are not unlikely. Children should be coached how to look for a way around obstacles when they occur.

If you have ever watched a child — perhaps a 5 or 6 year old — learn a computer game on his own, you know that young children have a natural ability to learn, undaunted, from their "mistakes." When they encounter obstacles, they simply keep trying different methods until they are successful. But somehow, during the school-age years, we adults have taught our children to dread making mistakes, that there is only one "correct" way to reach a goal and that "grades" are the measure of a person's worth. *There is a need to change the way children think about making mistakes, asking questions, and addressing tasks and problems in our schools.* This is much more than just another paragraph in my writing about education—this is a big deal.

An analytical approach to communications.

Certainly we must help children develop good listening, note making, grammar, vocabulary, speech and writing skills. More than these are required, however, to avoid misunderstanding and disadvantage by way of misinformation or insufficient information. Whether sending or receiving information, a person should make a real-time, analytical, internal audit to enhance the likelihood of a complete and appropriate communication. Another "mental buffet" of questions should be called upon when receiving information. A sampler might include the following:

- Do I understand this?
- Does this address the core of the issue?
- What is missing? What else do I need to know?
- Is this compatible with other information I already know to be correct?

The results of this analysis dictate the questions and comments the receiver must issue to ensure effective communication. Similarly, someone who is sending an oral or written communication should, when appropriate, first consult his mental buffet:

- What does the listener/reader need to know?
- How can I say/write this in a cogent way?
- Will the listener/reader understand this?
- What other considerations are there besides articulation and understanding?
- What questions and disagreements can I anticipate and prepare for?

These communication skills can be taught and learned as surely as other communication skills can. It is simply a matter of our initiative.

A team orientation.

"Teamwork" is largely an adult concept. However, by the time youngsters reach high school, many of them are able to understand that an athletic team's success will in no small way depend upon the degree to which its members cooperate. Even the middle school years can offer opportunities for youngsters to learn to work cooperatively on class projects and tasks.

Children should be given real-life, hands-on experiences (some in school and others extending beyond school into the community) which help them learn that

- two heads (and two sets of hands) are usually better than one;
- teamwork requires good communications;
- teamwork requires open-mindedness, give and take, and respect for others' views;
- teamwork requires organization, planning, and goals;
- teamwork requires your best effort at making a meaningful contribution;
- each member of the team has something to contribute, will make mistakes, and has areas to improve upon;
- we are social beings and we are interdependent;
- it is important for each member of the team to understand other members' jobs in order for anticipation and trouble-shooting to be facilitated;
- the overall outcome will largely reflect how well the members worked together; and personal and group satisfaction should be derived in large measure from the notion that "it's not whether you won or lost, but how you played the game."

In the face of increasing competitiveness and the need to get more done in less time with better quality, many businesses have come to emphasize teamwork as the most sensible way to get things done. And the benefits of teamwork are no less potent in our homes and communities. It falls to our schools to help children develop a team orientation, and every class in every subject affords opportunities for this development.

A service attitude.

Some of our youths today seem to be "out for themselves" rather than being concerned about the welfare or opinions of someone else. This posture is incompatible with a basic requirement in the workplace today, where terms like "customer service" and "customer orientation" have become more important than ever before. And "customers" are not limited to people who purchase a product.

In the workplace, anyone an individual works with is, in a way, a customer; too, customer relationships exist between groups and between departments within an organization. These relationships, when they function properly, are characterized by

- an understanding of the other person's job and how it fits in to the larger picture;
- awareness of the other person's point of view and circumstances;
- respect for the other person's opinions and feelings;
- a spirit of trust, cooperation, good deeds and good will;
- a demonstrated concern for the best interests of the other person, in balance with one's own best interests;
- a genuine, best effort given on a task, with attention to the best possible quality;
- interpersonal sincerity; and
- a dedication to effective communications.

Businesses have learned that a service attitude on the part of employees is in everyone's best interests, from employee morale to company profits. In fact, this is a matter of common sense with far-reaching applications. Our schools should look for every opportunity to help children develop this attribute, as individuals and as groups, within the school and without.

Receptiveness for new challenges.

If you get children out of their textbooks for a while, if you give them new experiences that are challenging but also interesting, if you get them involved with activities that are fun at best and practical (in the youngster's view) at least, then you have paved the way for the best kind of learning possible.

The idea here is to lay out a smorgasbord of broadening, age-appropriate experiences for children—experiences that are "hands-on," real-life, and applied or practical in nature. Some of these experiences should be mandatory, while others may be chosen from a group. Some may be seminars and demonstrations lasting one class period, while others may be units lasting a week or perhaps a grading period. While school personnel, including administrators, may present or coordinate these experiences, many of them should involve individuals from outside the school system.

This educational style is quite effective because the "learning" part of it is hidden or compensated for by the interest the child has in the experience. While a given activity may be fun or exciting, it is essential that it not be a passive experience for the youngster. Indeed, the real challenge for the teacher is to build the development of specific skills and knowledge right into the experience. Too, it is important that there be a measurable product or end result of the experience whether on an individual or group basis.

Mathematics and writing are examples of skills that can be required of youngsters in order for them to reach a desired goal. If someone outside the system is involved, the teacher should work closely with that person to ensure that much more than entertainment will take place. The teacher's role here would be to co-develop a plan of action designed with learning objectives built in.

Consider a requirement that in the eighth or ninth grade all students take a woodshop class (lasting perhaps a grading period) which introduces them to basic tools, safe procedures, wood characteristics, and the planning and execution of a shop project. All students would be required to make a small box as a final outcome or product of the experience. They would be able to choose their own type(s) of wood to use, choose from several designs (or design their own), and choose a stain and finish, as well as hardware.

In the process, students will have to follow directions, make some decisions, lay out a plan, use arithmetic, measure accurately, give attention to detail, follow safety rules, meet deadlines, cooperate with others, learn about tools, learn from their mistakes (and discover that everybody else makes mistakes, too), and be persevering.

It cannot realistically be done? It was part of the eighth grade curriculum for me in public school around 1960, and it was a great learning experience. Such esteem-building learning experiences can and must be provided to our children.

In the ninth grade we studied orthographics (great for deductive reasoning) in our metal shop class. Yes, orthographics in ninth grade public school. And, yes, metal shop, including a forge, oxyacetylene braising, welding, and cutting, spot welding, riveting, rolling, soldering, acid etching, and finishing of metals. What has happened since then to our expectations of a student's capacity to learn?

What follow are some other "subject" ideas for experiences in which I believe our schools should engage children. Some of these could be one-time experiences while others may be arranged in a sequence of increasingly challenging experiences. Many, if not most, of these should be mandatory elements in the school system curriculum.

Remember that many of these topics offer a great opportunity to integrate school with community:

- How to use and balance a checking account.
- Intelligent consumerism; analyzing the marketplace; planned purchases; critical analysis of commercial advertizing;
- How to make and use a family budget.
- Good manners; etiquette.

- How to make a good impression (eye contact, shaking hands, appearance...).
- How to read/use a newspaper.
- How to handle tax forms.
- How to repair things in the home.
- How to save money for the future; make investments; plan for retirement.
- The etymology of words and phrases.
- Community service activities; helping to resolve community problems/needs.
- Basic cooking (soups, salads, breads, roasts, breakfasts,...) for family meals—Everyone should know how to cook good food.
- Current events and issues (world-wide to local); civic awareness and involvement.
- How to use credit wisely; borrowing money.
- How to make notes, outline, locate resources, study for a test (we had a grading-period length class in high school).
- How to select and apply for college.
- How to seek employment.
- Insurance for health, car, life.
- Division of labor; responsibilities at home/school/community; teamwork.
- Intelligent argument; resolving interpersonal conflict; extemporaneous debate.
- Mineral chemistry (as an extension of chemistry class); fascinating!
- Astrophysics and quantum physics (as an extension of physics class).
- Planning/organizing a small business.
- Basic economics (in the home, community; our national economy, markets; world economics).

- Examine change (technological, social, family, legal, governmental, economic...) for trends, impact, coping techniques, and even guiding change itself.
- Swimming lessons.
- Comparative religions.
- Planning a trip.
- This list is endless!

Once a child's interest has been stimulated in a subject, we can begin to release the great potential for learning that lies within the child. And once a child's mindset or attitude about new and challenging subject matter has been opened up and made receptive, there is almost no limit to the learning that can take place over time.

I have seen some of these topics presented as one-shot exposures to limited groups of students, which is but a small step in the right direction. And I have seen other "enrichment" programs limited to students who are deemed gifted or high achievers—programs that *all* students should be exposed to.

Is it asking too much of our teachers to stimulate wonder and curiosity and to teach children how to learn? Certainly, the easiest form of teaching involves "fast-food teachers" who are content to present pre-packaged information to students and then measure student performance on the basis of unthoughtful regurgitation on tests they have had to be taught how to take. I realize the style of teaching I am advocating here requires great energy, drive, innovation/creativity, flexibility, patience, perseverance and no less important, receptivity to children—the ability to learn from them and care what they think about.

The challenges of such a teaching style are far from beyond our capabilities, however. Teachers who do not know how to implement programs like these can be trained to do so. Teachers who are untrainable should be dismissed after having had an opportunity to perform. If suitable training programs are not available in the marketplace, the school system should develop its own—and why not?

Chapter 9

Let's Talk About Right and Wrong

In beautiful harmony, the chorus refrain chants
"I want it all. I want it all. I want it all. And I want it now!"
Another modern commercial advertisement
targeting our youths.
—An unfortunate sign of the times...

It is probably safe to suggest that many years ago our schools incorporated a much higher level of instruction about values, respect, and good and bad behavior than they do today. No doubt due to its association with religious doctrine, this exposure has been gradually removed from the classroom. And I agree that while the classroom is a good place to study various religions, it is not a good place for religious practice or promotion.

Serious problems began to develop, however, when we became afraid of talking with our children in the classroom about what is good and bad and what is right and wrong. It seemed to come to the point that even to refer to something in those terms would be to draw the wrath of someone or some group with the claim that religious dogma was being taught or that no one has the right to decide what is right and wrong for someone else. Consequently, a morals void seems to have developed, and newspaper editorials about the "rudderless value development" of our children have appeared as warnings worth our attention.

Another byproduct of this void of traditional moral standards has been the prominence of situational ethics and self-interest. Thus, the end justifies the means with more frequency today, and there is more interest in taking care of "number one" first at the expense of others—more interest, too, in satisfying our immediate wants, with an insufficient concern for the future.

There is a real need to take definite steps to instill right-thinking and good values in our children. Success will not be achieved upon the efforts of the school system alone, but there is much the schools can do to get things started. I have a few suggestions for you to consider after I specify some values I believe to be worthy of our educational programs:

- Respect for other people -- for their feelings, their age and experiences, their authority, their opinions.
- Good will, kindness and courtesy over negativism, hurtfulness and rudeness.
- A sense of responsibility for one's actions and inactions. By example, *if it is the teacher's responsibility to provide quality instruction, it is the student's responsibility to learn.*
- Respect for the environment, for nature, for life.
- Cleanliness and neatness for one's self, room, home, and community.
- Helpfulness and service to others.
- Respect for property, whether one's own or someone else's. Things should be properly taken care of.
- A best effort should be made with a given task, which should be completed properly and on time.

- Teamwork and cooperation over being "out for yourself" only.
- Commitment to doing what was promised; to one's family; to one's job; to doing the right thing.
- Effective communication and understanding over misunderstanding, poor grammar and speech, foul language, and ignorance of a complete truth.
- Foresight, good planning, goal-setting, and a sense of purpose and of mission, rather than procrastination, aimlessness, and living for immediate gratification.
- Self-discipline as a key to success, while losing control to anger or lethargy lead one toward failure.
- Fairness and justice as a vital ingredient in the glue that holds any group of people together in harmony.
- Learning and education as personally life-enriching; as a path to a successful, happy life; as something which advances the whole of society.
- Integrity and honor over lying, cheating, stealing, and taking undue advantage of others for personal gain.
- Leadership by example and by quality performance rather than leadership by winning and by appearances; confidence should be tempered by humility.

Of course, no one is perfect! The "good values" I have listed above should be held before our youths by the adults in their lives as worthy, personal goals of character to *strive for* on a daily basis. But the adults must be striving, also, lest their hypocrisy undermine the whole effort. Good values should be deliberately promulgated at every opportunity. What follow are some ideas that come to mind as to how this effort could be launched in our schools:

1. Teachers should look for and take every opportunity to engage students in *dialogue* about values and moral issues that

present themselves. Issues could range from cheating on a test to an incident of rudeness; from poor sportsmanship to dropping a small piece of trash in the hall; from stealing to inappropriate dress; from indolence to procrastination. If the issue distinguishes bad from good, no incident is too small to receive at least some attention from an adult in the school. Judgment should be exercised to determine if the dialogue and counseling should be a class exercise, individually handled on the side, or made in the form of a referral to a specialist. Athletic coaches have an equal share of this responsibility. Where better to set forth the notions that excellent performance and fun in an athletic event are more important than winning; that teamwork is more worthy than showing-off; that self-control is productive, while anger is destructive; and that providing a best effort builds self-esteem? A teacher or coach need not have a PhD in psychology in order to provide guidance which draws upon the basic sense of right and wrong to be found within each of us.

2. In addition to providing a philosophical treatment of types of governments (totalitarian through libertarian), a required high school class in government should focus upon the formation and development of our own government. The civics aspect of this subject, beginning with a study of the Declaration of Independence and the Constitution of the United States with its Amendments, offers fertile ground for dialogue about the values that shaped our nation. All of this could build to the importance of civic involvement and informed voting in contemporary society. Could we use student government to bring this to life?

3. Community involvement and service should be promoted by the school system. A full menu of activities could be developed to include such projects as picking up trash; facilitating the recycling program; providing attention to the

elderly; coordinating a food program for the poor; conducting fund-raising to benefit worthy causes; and visiting the ill or handicapped who are confined to their homes or the hospital. These experiences would also provide the opportunity for some "hands-on" learning connected to the real world outside the classroom. Such programs could be partly voluntary and partly required with different activities used across different age groups as appropriate. This same concept could be applied within the school system itself, with older students tutoring and giving seminars to younger children. Indeed, school systems should consider perhaps 100 hours of community service as a high school graduation requirement.

4. A task force formed by the high school student leadership, a guidance counselor and a group of teachers should explore the value and feasibility of establishing an honor system (to include a student honor council) at the school. If it considered such a system desirable and possible, the task force could design it and oversee its implementation. Further, the student leadership could become involved with student discipline, for there is much more to learn about leadership than what is provided by being elected to an office and getting subordinates to coordinate some activities.

The school system should ensure that high academic and athletic achievements are not the only accomplishments that result in meaningful awards and recognition. Students who demonstrate exceptional responsibility, cooperation, sportsmanship, initiative, and good will (to name a few possibilities) should receive recognition, too.

There are a number of teachers in most school systems who value the character development of their students and have built in to their own instruction some steps to provide it. In many classes, however, this is only a piecemeal effort, as most teachers either do not know how to go about this or do not want to be bothered with yet another burden of responsibility, another set of daily hassles, and another source of stress.

A character education program, however, will be ineffective without the dedication of all adults across the entire school system. Inappropriate behavior simply must not be tolerated; worthy behavior must at least be recognized; and *we must not refrain from discussing issues of character* with our children, however large or small the incident. Every time we "look the other way" we perform a disservice to our children and contribute to the long-range ills of our society at large.

Chapter 10

Our Moral Imperative

"It takes a village to raise a child."
– Just another empty slogan.

This chapter will close the series I have written regarding my concerns about education. In it, I wish to point to my belief that while our problems in education are serious and complex, they are surmountable, given the exercise of responsible citizenship within the large and small communities of America.

There can be no question about the magnitude of our education woes. There has been a steady stream of reports under credible authorship over the last four decades to indicate on the whole that our schools need to be doing a much better job in preparing our youths (and our nation) for a successful future. Even recent reports indicate severe problems which reveal themselves in the form of our lackluster academic standing among industrialized nations, high drop-out rates, high rates of functional illiteracy, and real trouble attracting and retaining quality teachers to the profession.

Other problems in our society (such as teen suicide, unwed teen pregnancies, drug dependency, and criminal activity) have found their way into our schools. As regrettable as these problems are, our schools have no choice but to deal with them as well as they can. Those who argue against the gravity of both the academic and social issues in education today are simply practicing denial.

Most of us who are concerned about education and get into discussions about it with friends generally develop a short list of the reasons for the problems we face in education. Here is such a list, in the form of a multiple choice question. Select the chief culprit:

A.   Poor parenting
B.   Weak teachers
C.   Inept school administrations
D.   Inadequate curriculums and methods of instruction
E.   Poor student discipline
F.   Apathetic communities
G.   Politicians (especially a do-little-of-value Congress)
H.   Incorrigible children
I.   Insufficient funding
J.   Minimal standards and expectations
K.   Ourselves, individually ("The enemy is *us!*")
L.   All of the above, and more

How could "L" not be the correct answer? However, that allows us the easy way out, doesn't it? For everyone nods in agreement when someone utters the famous slogan, "It takes a village to raise a child." The emptiness of this slogan appears, however, when we realize that it is everyone *else* in the village who we like to think will be responsible because… I am just so busy and what little I might do will not achieve much anyway. As a troublemaker in a crowd feels more secure due to his anonymity, so we can assuage our guilt by outsourcing responsibility for education upon the shoulders of "A" through "J." What pathetic lumps of flesh we are to neglect our children so! If you had to pick any one answer other than "L" wouldn't it have to be "K"?

If by accepting individual responsibility for the education of children we are at least looking in the correct direction, how can we begin to take some steps to effect solutions? We should first revisit the "village" that must raise our children, examine what values must drive our actions, and determine how we interact with each other to achieve our goals.

Obviously, (1) there are no simple or quick solutions, (2) there are no guidebooks and no canned programs that have been developed that a school system can use to implement improvements (*this writing included*), (3) we cannot expect to be saved by grand programs generated by the Federal or state governments, and (4) our school systems cannot by themselves surmount the problems that beset education today.

To begin to find solutions for problems holding us back from educational excellence, we need to focus our attention at the community level. First, consider the relationships between a few of the fundamental elements of a community.

My impression is that at some point in the past, there was a fairly close link, with the possible exception of "employment," among the basic elements of our day-to-day living in America, perhaps thus:

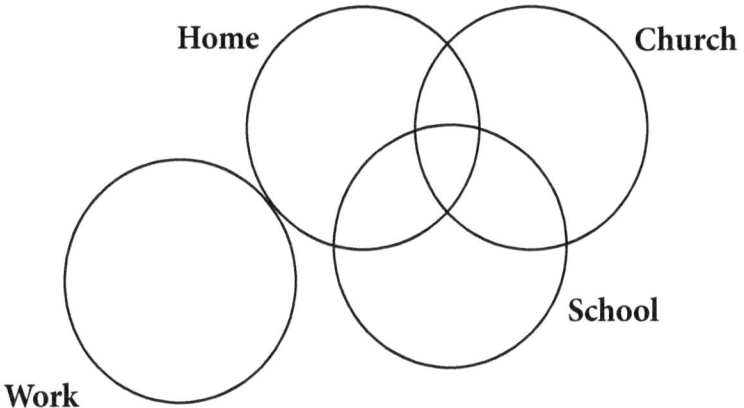

A literal notion of "community" comes to mind in considering the closer relationship that once existed among home, church and school.

Values originating in the church penetrated deeply into the home and school alike. Education was valued to the extent that teachers were highly respected by children, and there was much support for education in the home.

Over the years, however, these elements seem to have moved apart as in the next graphic.

Religious influences in the school have been withdrawn; accordingly, a void in values development has taken place within the educational institution. For many people, life has become much more complex and time-consuming than in the past. There is more pressure and difficulty now in trying to balance the needs associated with children, careers, property, rest and recreation, religion, community activities, and social engagements. In another area of the socioeconomic spectrum, it has become increasingly difficult to find work, have enough to eat, and keep a family together.

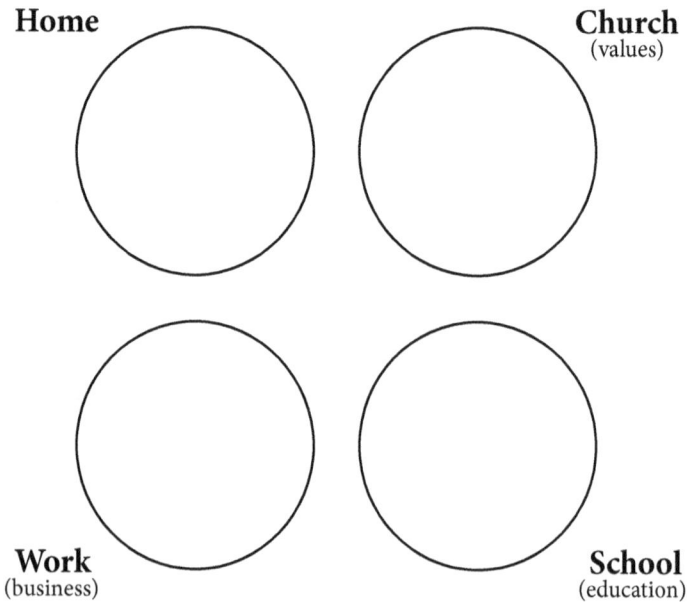

Home   **Church**
                                                  (values)

Work   **School**
(business)   (education)

Difficult decisions have had to be made in apportioning our attention to so many needs. And in the interests of some kind of economy of time, we have largely separated these areas of need, one from another. Accordingly, "education" is something that happens at school—the *schools* are wholly responsible for educating our children ("Isn't that what we pay our taxes for?"); religion is something that happens once a week in the church; many people, whether because of intrinsic or economic need, become intensely bound up with their work or career, often to the detriment of their "home life"; and so on, with an increasing need to "budget our time" for recreation and whatever else. Many do not even have time to eat breakfast in the morning or to get regular exercise even with the knowledge that such things are vital to good health and longevity.

And as we have separated/compartmentalized our needs, so also it seems we have become more distant from each other on matters of substance; for how often in the present age do we take time to sit down together and talk about truly important concerns and issues? It seems to me that our children have in large measure received short shrift with these changes in our lifestyle.

What I am proposing is that we rekindle our *sense of community* with education at its center, for the education of our children has become quintessential to the success (and perhaps the survival) of our society and of the human species.

Effective solutions must grow out of nothing less than a major crusade for educational excellence—a crusade that *develops at the local level* and cuts across all the major segments of the community. The process must start with a serious, ongoing dialogue, and it is the professionals at the front lines of education—the teachers—whose expertise should be sought out at an early stage and throughout the process.

Equally important would be the contributions of area businesses, parents, school administrators, colleges, local government, and religious and health institutions. The promise of such a partnership in education would be not only the success that grows out of it but also the satisfaction that results from such a grass-roots interactive involvement in the process.

Home ⬤ ⬤ **Values**
(via church
and character
develpment
curricula)

Education

**Local business,
government,
civic groups ...**

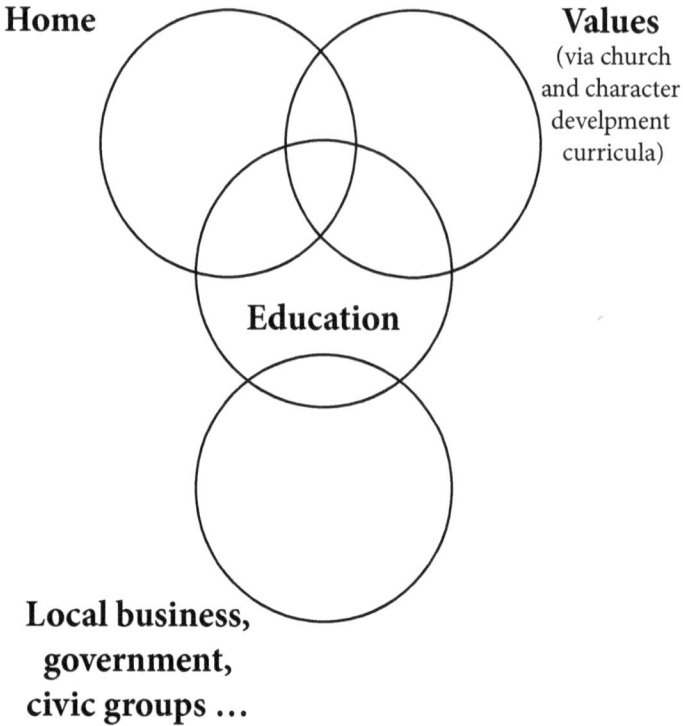

Solutions must begin and end with the schools. School administrators should open themselves up to and in fact solicit suggestions and meaningful involvement from their own professional staffs and from the community. Correspondingly, individuals and organizations in the community must take on a sense of responsibility for the education of the community's children and accordingly become actively involved—they must insert themselves into the process.

This joint venture could include (but not be limited to) tutoring, instructional support in the classroom, mentoring, seminars/workshops for students, training and developmental activities for school personnel, and task force activities to address such issues as curriculum development, student discipline, and compensation.

The tradition of blaming others for how conditions are and of looking to the past to find excuses for our defensiveness will not generate solutions for our children; instead, they will reinforce the status quo with all its divisiveness and accordant victimization of children. Interpersonal trust must be developed, and communication gaps must be closed for our children's sake. We must be vigilant in focusing always on cooperation that will benefit our children.

Key terms: children; future; positive mindset; cooperation; and selfless, constructive actions for a greater good.

There must be no "silent majority." One need not participate on a task force or in a tutoring program to make an important contribution. *Anyone* can correct rudeness, can insist that litter be picked up, can make sure that a child is attending school and completing schoolwork, can visit the halls and the classrooms of the school system to have a sense of what the learning environment is like, can offer a compliment to a good teacher, can commend a successful club sponsor (and even offer to help), can engage others in conversations about education, and so on.

In my notes I have presented you with my most pressing thoughts and feelings on educational issues. Remember to view my writing *simply as a starting place for dialogue at the community level.* By way of thoughtful brainstorming and pluck, the potential for cooperation, goodwill, and significant achievement would seem to be limitless. Indeed, the by-products of a community effort such as this could be as rewarding as the goal. Think of it as an education barnraising!

Let's see… How did those barnraisings work? Was the work done by a handful of leaders or by a significant portion of the available population with each member of a diverse group performing whatever it was and at whatever level he could to make a contribution? What was more important—individual agendas or a common goal that unified everyone? And when it came time to raise someone else's barn, what loomed larger—everyone's own day-to-day schedules and needs, or a spirit of community coupled with the knowledge that we are profoundly interdependent in this life? If we do not self-sacrifice to help each other, we may immediately advantage ourselves as individuals, but we are all ultimately doomed.

Whether in the case of a barnraising or a much larger, more complex effort such as is suggested by this writing, the project requires authority, a plan, organization, leadership, and the support of at least a critical mass of affected and involved individuals even to get it started.

This suggests that the leadership of a given community, such as a city council, must recognize the merit of such a project and approve productive, autonomous action on the part of some kind of education czar-team composed of representatives from diverse groups across the community, each with a vested interest in education. Such a team could be composed of individuals from any of the following: the school board, the city council, the teachers, the PTA, the Chamber of Commerce, the Economic Development Commission, the local newspaper, legal counsel, social services, and a unified church organization.

The chief purpose of such a lead team would be to draw upon its connections with several key elements of the community to facilitate, coordinate, and enable actions, most of which would be executed by subordinate teams. The lead team would be held accountable by a constant exposure to the public, perhaps best through occasional public forums on specific topics and active reporting by the local newspaper about progress made by the teams and about status reports and reactions from the teaching community, the parent community, the church community, and such.

One of the operative terms above regarding the lead team is "autonomous," meaning that once this team receives authority from the governmental leadership of the community, it should not operate under the thumb of any one constituency—including the city council itself and the school board. While there will be many actions that can be decided on and accomplished at lower levels (such as within a particular school, within social services, within the church community, within the PTA,...) and not subject to specific approval by, say, the school board or city council, there will be other actions to be recommended to a proper authority for approval—all under a better-informed public eye.

And when the inevitable brick wall of state or Federal requirements becomes an obstacle to progress with a particular action, it falls to local government to petition in the strongest terms and through every means available on behalf of its children. Even failing in the effort, let it not be said of any community that no effort was attempted by its own government to overcome resistance to a worthy need, to right a wrong, or to insist on foresightfulness over the natural tradition of myopia.

Doesn't the magnitude of this need and what it will take to address it seem overwhelming? Very naturally it does. But it crept insidiously upon us over many years and is a well-entrenched scourge upon our children's future. This, unlike other threats in our history (such as any war, the Great Depression, the Dust Bowl era, and the Sputnik challenge—which prompted tremendous improvements in education) that more suddenly warranted extraordinary leadership and effort on the part of the powerful and the everyday citizenry alike.

Thus, we must realize that the current state of education in the United States is every bit as threatening to us as the threats that more suddenly and dramatically developed long ago, and it warrants action on our part that is no less urgent and significant than what was necessary before. But with disappointing results coming out of Washington, it falls to us at the local level to take action and garner state-level support as best we can.

We must not allow the day-to-day pressures and constraints in our lives to prevent us from giving our children the resources they need to build a successful future for themselves. If we fail to fulfill our responsibilities, our children will be hindered in fulfilling theirs. In the circumstances of the present age, providing quality education is more than our responsibility—providing quality education is our moral imperative.

The fact of the matter is we all have to behave in a way
that's better than what comes naturally to us.
—Andy Rooney

We invite you to view the complete
selection of titles we publish at:

www.TEACHServices.com

Scan with your mobile
device to go directly
to our website.

Please write or e-mail us your praises, reactions, or
thoughts about this or any other book we publish at:

TEACH Services, Inc.
P U B L I S H I N G
www.TEACHServices.com ● (800) 367-1844

P.O. Box 954
Ringgold, GA 30736

info@TEACHServices.com

TEACH Services, Inc., titles may be purchased in bulk for
educational, business, fund-raising, or sales promotional use.
For information, please e-mail:

BulkSales@TEACHServices.com

Finally, if you are interested in seeing
your own book in print, please contact us at

publishing@TEACHServices.com

We would be happy to review your manuscript for free.

www.ingramcontent.com/pod-product-compliance
Lightning Source LLC
Chambersburg PA
CBHW060553100426
42742CB00013B/2548